Facts About the Mexican Red Knee Tarantula

By Lisa Strattin

© 2016 Lisa Strattin

Revised © 2019

Facts for Kids Picture Books by Lisa Strattin

Harlequin Macaw, Vol 34

Downy Woodpecker, Vol 37

Frilled Lizard, Vol 39

Purple Finch, Vol 48

Poison Dart Frogs, Vol 50

Giant Otter, Vol 57

Hornbill, Vol 67

Dwarf Lemur, Vol 73

Giant Squirrel, Vol 76

Star Tortoise, Vol 79

Sign Up for New Release Emails Here

http://LisaStrattin.com/subscribe-here

Monthly Surprise Box

http://KidCraftsByLisa.com

All rights reserved. No part of this book may be reproduced by any means whatsoever without the written permission from the author, except brief portions quoted for purpose of review.

All information in this book has been carefully researched and checked for factual accuracy. However, the author and publisher makes no warranty, express or implied, that the information contained herein is appropriate for every individual, situation or purpose and assume no responsibility for errors or omissions. The reader assumes the risk and full responsibility for all actions, and the author will not be held responsible for any loss or damage, whether consequential, incidental, special or otherwise, that may result from the information presented in this book.

All images are free for use or purchased from stock photo sites for commercial use.

Some coloring pages might be of the general species due to lack of available images.

I have relied on my own observations as well as many different sources for this book and I have done my best to check facts and give credit where it is due. In the event that any material is used without proper permission, please contact me so that the oversight can be corrected.

Contents

INTRODUCTION 7

CHARACTERISTICS 9

APPEARANCE 11

LIFE STAGES 13

LIFE SPAN 15

SIZE 17

HABITAT 19

DIET 21

FRIENDS AND ENEMIES 23

SUITABILITY AS PETS 25

TARANTULA MODEL 38

MONTHLY SURPRISE BOX 39

INTRODUCTION

Mexican red-knee tarantulas are large spiders that live in Mexico. They live in a wide range of habitats from deserts to tropical forest. They are arthropods and have eight legs. They are slow growing and shed their exoskeleton to grow.

They are venomous and they use their venom to help them catch their food. They eat mostly insects and can help keep some insect populations from getting out of control. They live in burrows usually found at the base of cacti.

Mexican red-knee tarantulas are tame and do not usually harm or attack people. They are kept in many zoos. Because they readily mate in captivity, they are often kept as pets.

CHARACTERISTICS

Mexican red-knee tarantulas live in burrows in rocky areas at the base of vegetation, usually a cactus, and they will ambush their prey from these burrows. Females live longer than male spiders. Females will also attack and sometimes kill male spiders after mating.

They have eight eyes that allow them to see forward and backwards. Despite having eight eyes they do not see very well and rely on the hairs on their legs to sense vibrations of prey as they walk by their burrows. They have special hairs on their two front legs they use to hold onto prey as they drag their prey into their home burrows. They are also able to taste and smell with special organs on their two front legs.

Mexican red-knee tarantulas are calm and do not attack people. However, if people threaten the spiders, they can throw small barbed hairs off of their stomachs to discourage people from getting too close. If they bite a person, it feels like a bee sting and it is not usually life threatening.

APPEARANCE

Mexican red-knee tarantulas are large, dark spiders with bright coloring on their legs. They have a black colored stomach and a light brown color going around their backs. They have a dark black square on the middle of their backs.

Their legs are covered with small hairs. The joints of each leg are bright orange to red in color. This is where the spiders get their name.

LIFE STAGES

Mexican red-knee tarantulas have three life stages. The first life stage is the egg. This life stage begins after males and females mate. The spiders mate in the fall during the rainy season (usually between July and October). The female spider then carries the sperm all winter and lays eggs on a special spider web in the spring. The female spider will carry the eggs around in her mouth between her fangs until they hatch. The eggs hatch in one to three months.

Once the eggs hatch, the juvenile life stage begins. Juvenile spiders will shed their exoskeleton (a support structure on the outside of their body like crabs) a lot during the first few weeks. Then their growth slows down and they shed their exoskeleton less frequently. They will move out of the burrow and live on their own after about two weeks, but they do not reach the final stage, adult stage, for four years in males and six years in females.

LIFE SPAN

There is not a lot of information on how long Mexican red-knee tarantulas live in the wild. In captivity male spiders live around five years on average, but have been reported to live as long as 10 years. Females live to an average of 25 years in captivity, but have been recorded to live as long as 30 years.

SIZE

Mexican red-knee tarantulas are large spiders. They are five to 5 ½ inches long on average. Female spiders have a bigger body than males, but male spiders have longer legs. Their leg span can be six to seven inches long. They can weigh up to 1/2 an ounce.

HABITAT

Mexican red-knee tarantulas are most often found in dry areas with little vegetation, but they can also be found in tropical forest. They only live in Mexico in the wild and make their burrows in rocky locations. Their burrows have one entrance and two chambers. One chamber is used for when the spider sheds its exoskeleton and the other chamber is used to store their left over food.

DIET

Mexican red-knee tarantulas eat a large variety of food items. They will primarily feed on large insects, but can also eat frogs and mice. They catch their food by hiding in their burrows and waiting until they feel a prey item walking past. Then they will quickly come out and grab their prey and drag it back into the burrow.

Mexican red-knee tarantulas will then bite their prey and inject it with venom. This will paralyze and turn the insides of the prey into a liquid. The spiders then drink the liquid and wrap the rest of the prey in a web and store it in their burrows.

FRIENDS AND ENEMIES

Mexican red-knee tarantulas do not have very many friends. They do not even get along with other spiders and will often attack spiders that walk near their burrows.

Mexican red-knee tarantulas have many enemies. Birds, moths, and lizards will all attack and eat these spiders. When a Mexican red-knee tarantula is attacked it will stand on its back legs and show its fangs to scare off the attacker. They will also throw small sharp hairs from their stomachs at the attacker. This helps the spider retreat to its burrow to escape.

Mexican red-knee tarantulas are also attacked by a special wasp. This wasp will sting the spider and paralyze it. Then the wasp will make a nest out of the spider's body and lay eggs. After the eggs hatch, the young wasp will eat the spider.

SUITABILITY AS PETS

Mexican red-knee tarantulas are often kept as pets. They can readily mate in captivity and can be found at most pet stores. They can be kept in a 10-gallon aquarium or terrarium as an enclosure. There needs to be a locking screen on top of the enclosure so that the spider cannot escape. Then there needs to be about two inches of dirt in the bottom and a little bowl with water. They can be fed small insects like crickets and meal worms that can be purchased in a pet store.

COLOR ME

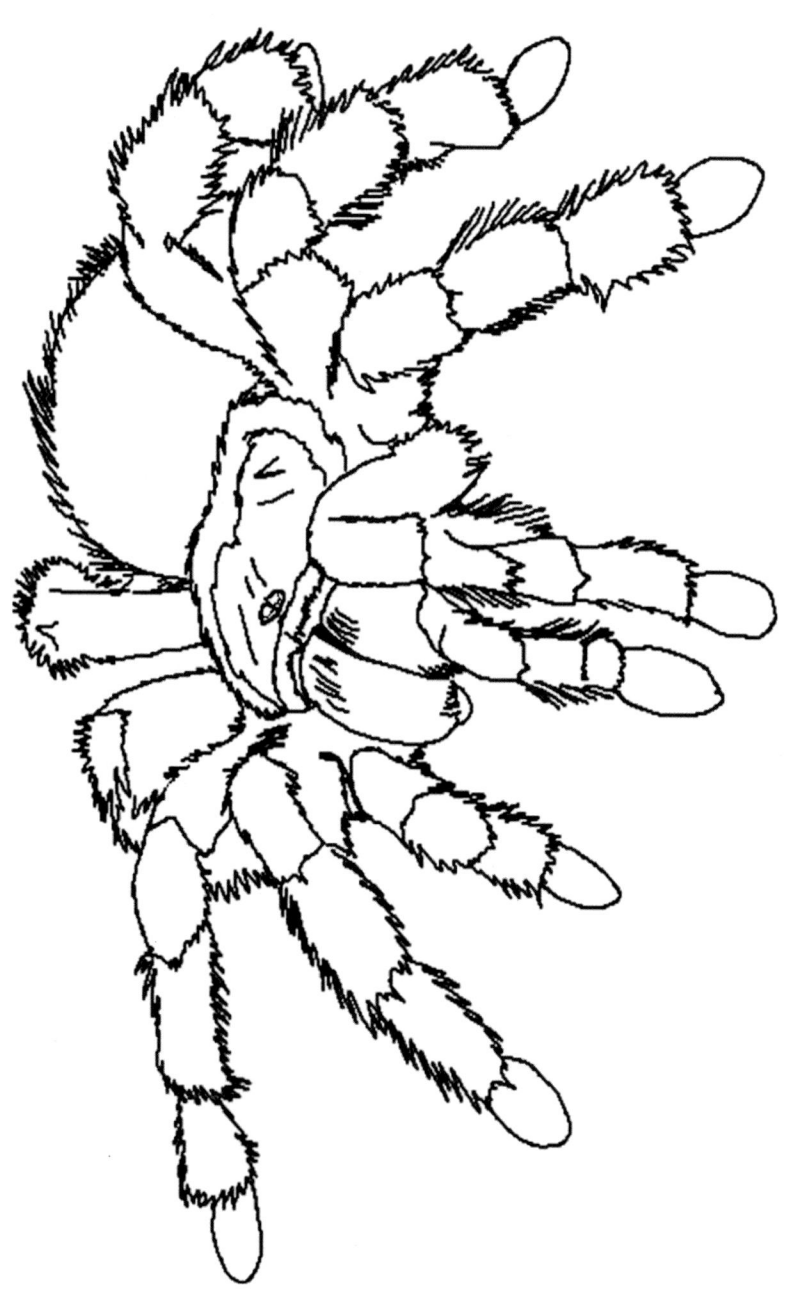

COLOR ME

COLOR ME

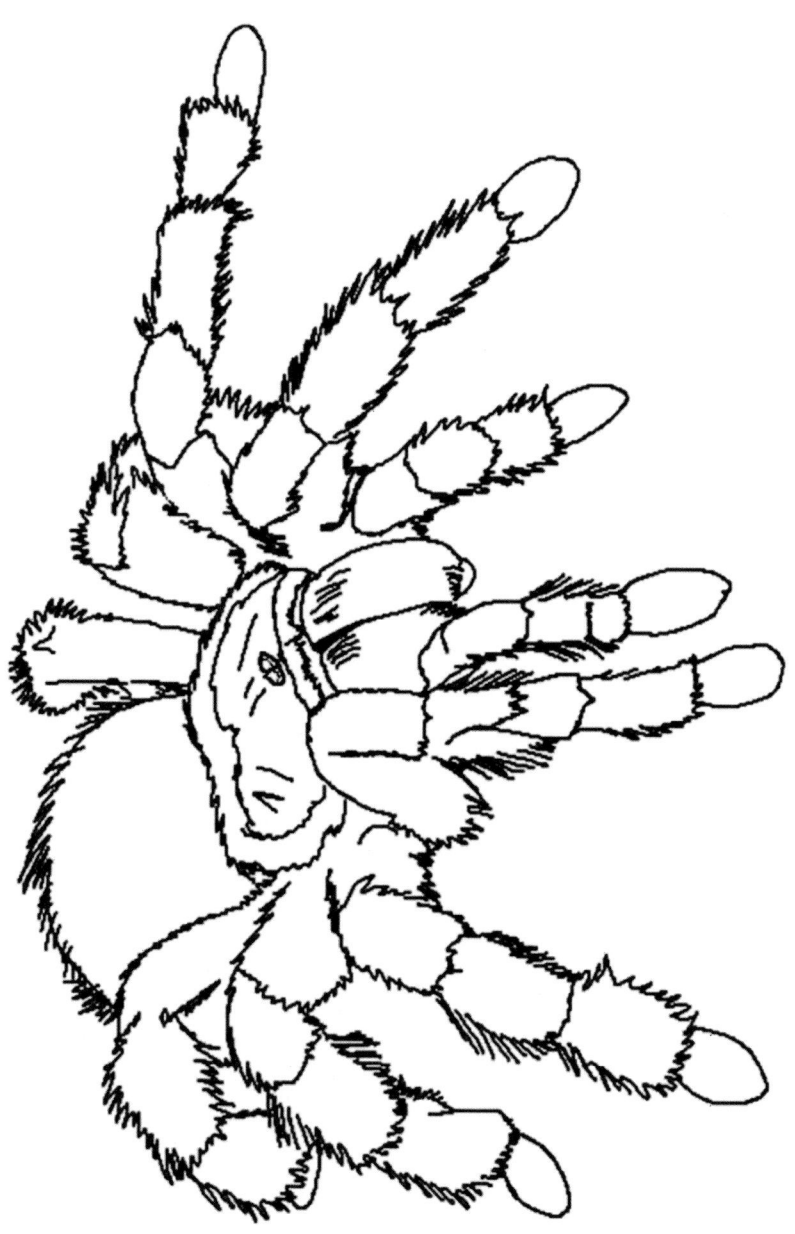

COLOR ME

COLOR ME

COLOR ME

COLOR ME

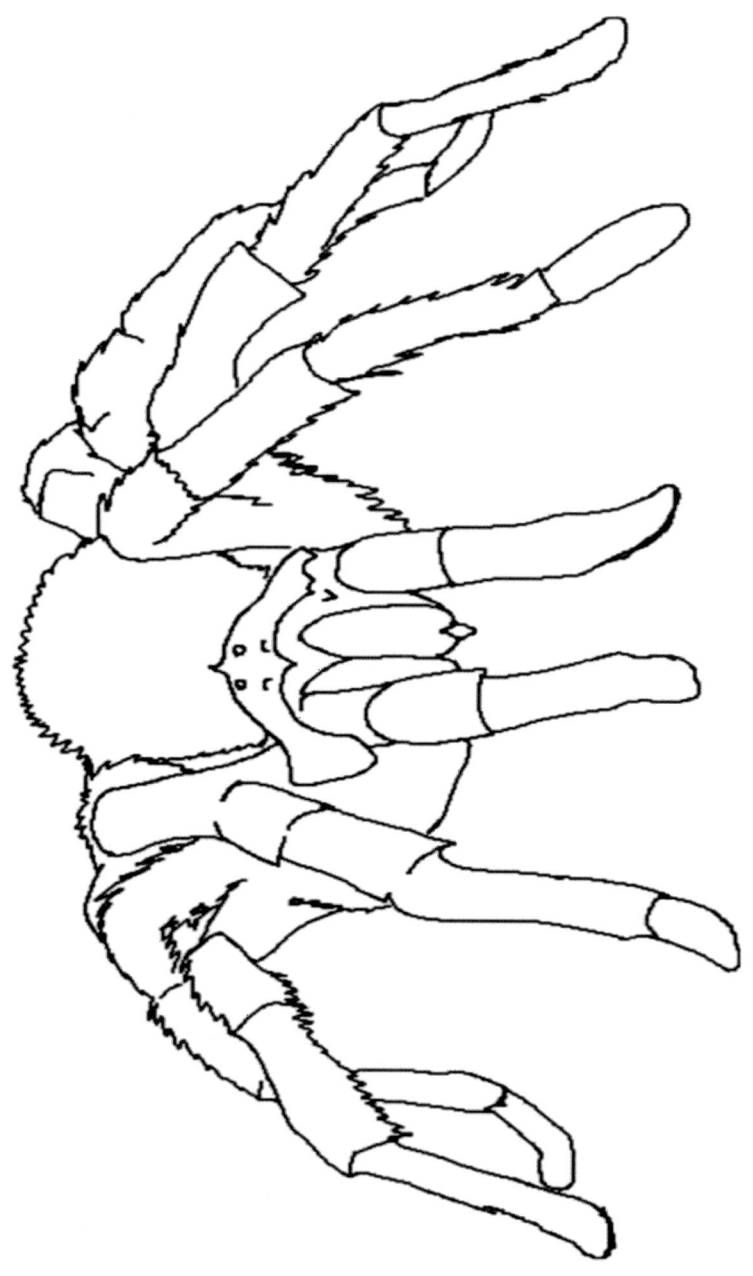

COLOR ME

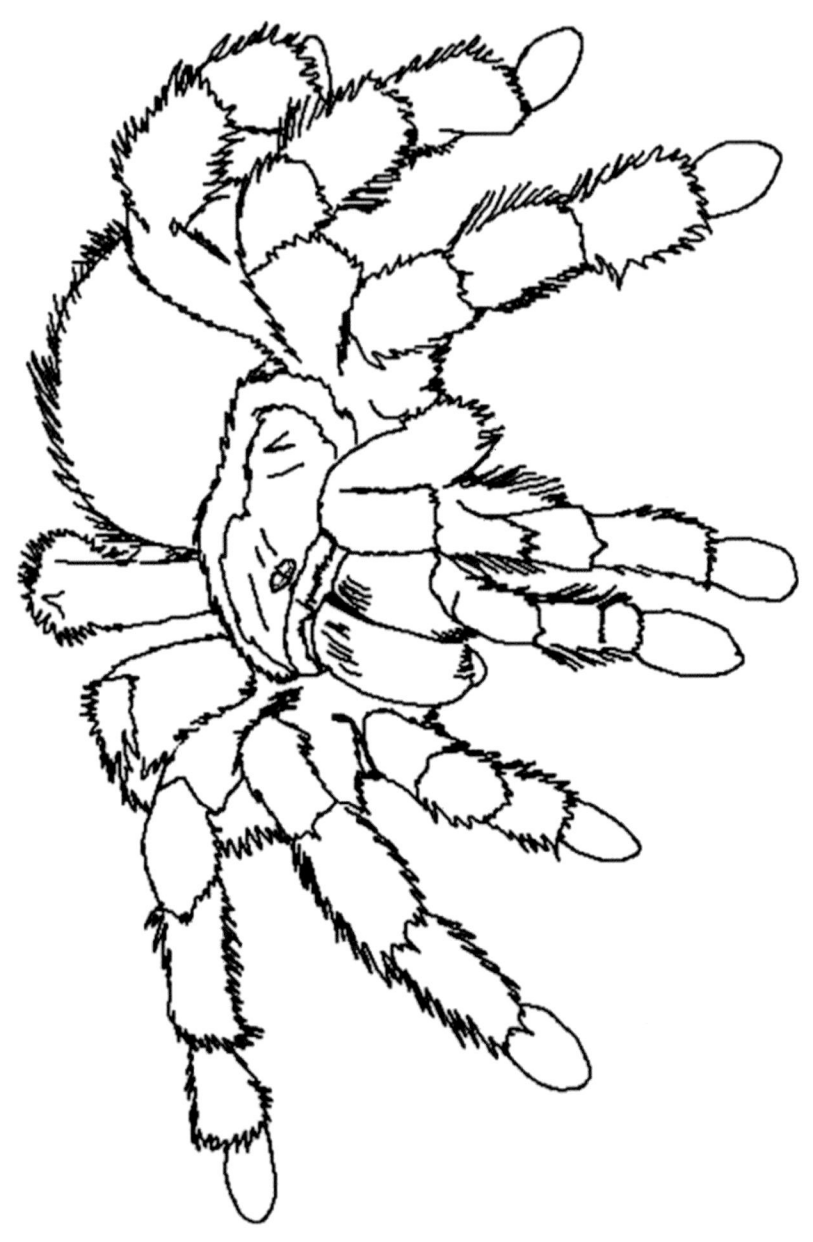

COLOR ME

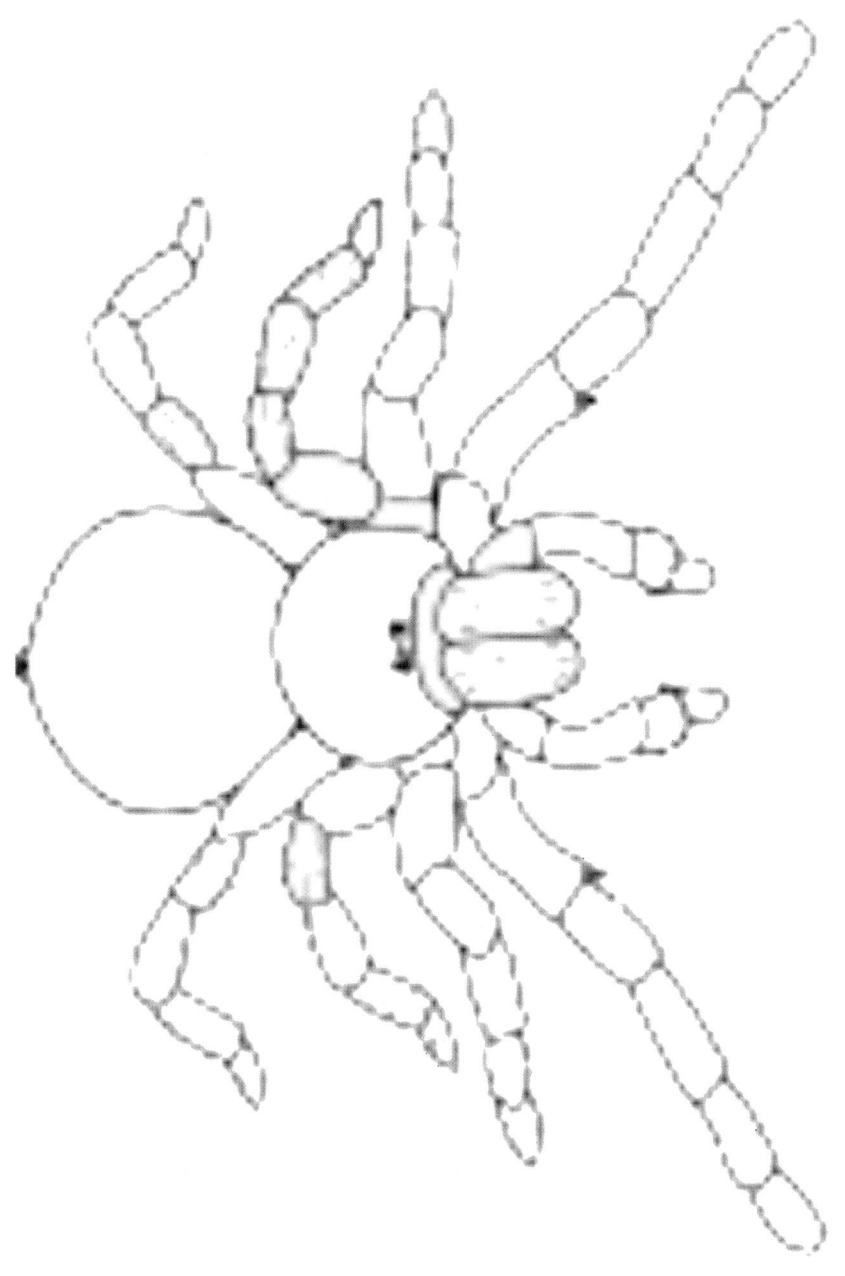

COLOR ME

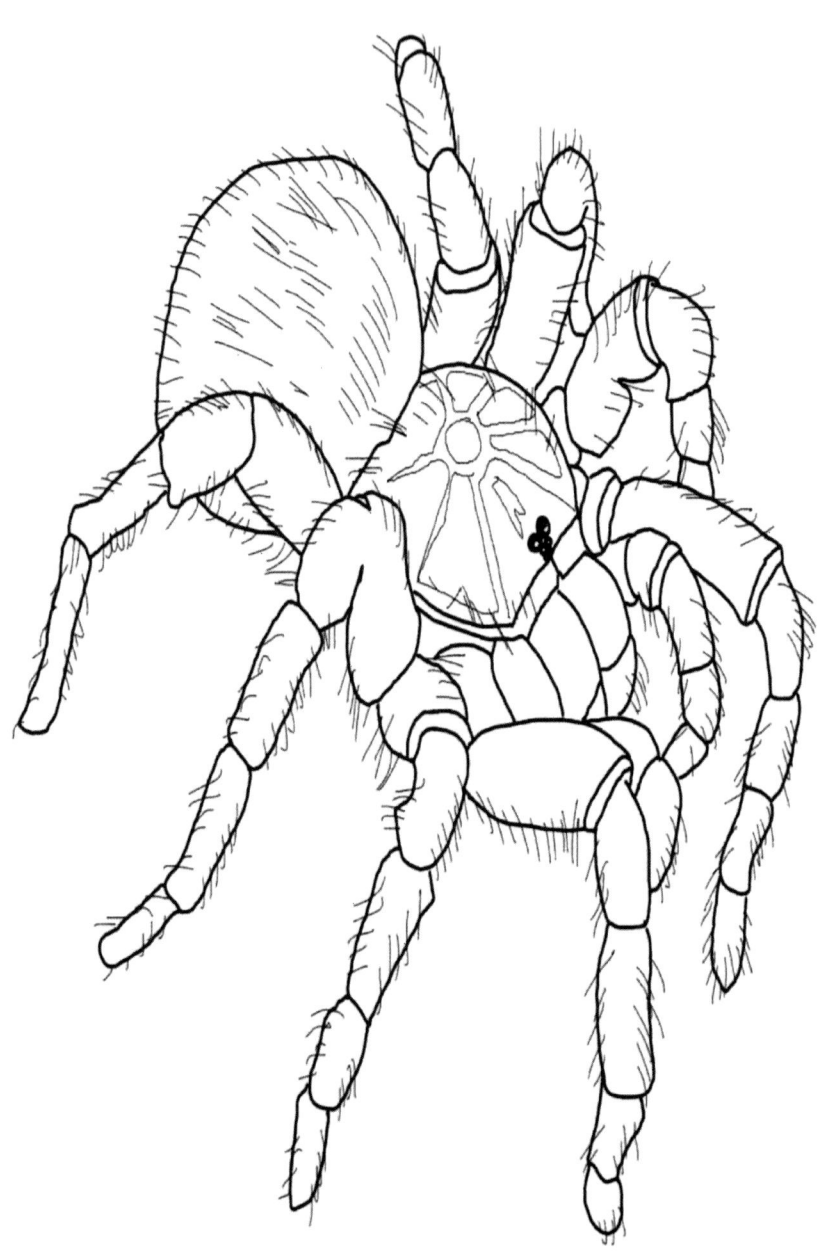

Please leave me a review here:

http://lisastrattin.com/Review-Vol-98

For more Kindle Downloads Visit Lisa Strattin Author Page on Amazon Author Central

http://amazon.com/author/lisastrattin

To see upcoming titles, visit my website at LisaStrattin.com– all books available on kindle!

http://lisastrattin.com

TARANTULA MODEL

You can get one by copying and pasting this link into your browser:

http://lisastrattin.com/tarantulamodel

MONTHLY SURPRISE BOX

Get yours by copying and pasting this link into your browser

http://KidCraftsByLisa.com

Made in the USA
Monee, IL
11 September 2020